This book belongs to

____

____

and I am finding out
about Jesus

Published by
Lion Hudson Limited
Wilkinson House, Jordan Hill Business Park,
Banbury Road, Oxford OX2 8DR, England
www.lionhudson.com

ISBN 978 1 78128 103 1
e-ISBN 978 1 78128 119 2

First edition 2014

Previously published in the UK by Scripture Union

Acknowledgments
Scripture taken from the Contemporary English Version.
Copyright © 1991, 1992, 1995 by American Bible Society.
Used by permission.

A catalogue record for this book is available from the British Library

Printed and bound in China,
August 2019, LH54

Would you like to know JESUS?

by Graham Jefferson and Eira Reeves
Illustrated by Eira Reeves

CANDLE BOOKS

God made lots of people.

God loves people everywhere –
grown-ups and children...

... and you.

God loves you and wants to be your best friend.

God sent his Son Jesus
to show us how to be
friends with him.

God wants his friends to be kind and loving and obedient.

But often we are unkind, unloving, and disobedient. That stops us being friends with God.

Jesus took the punishment for
the wrong things we have done.
He died on the cross for us.

After Jesus died he came alive again. Then he went back to heaven to be with his Father God.

Jesus is still alive!
In a wonderful way he can be with us now – whatever we're doing.

Would you like to know Jesus?

This is what you
need to do…

First talk to Jesus as you would
talk to a friend.
This is called praying.

Say "I'm sorry" to him for all the wrong things you have done.

Sometimes we need to say
"I'm sorry" to other friends too.

Thank Jesus for loving you.
Ask him to come and be your friend
for always...

… and he will!

Here is a prayer.

Every day talk to Jesus.
Tell him when you're happy and
when you're sad. Find out more
about your friend Jesus in the Bible.

Ask your family if you can go to Sunday school. You may attend one already – that's good.

Now have a really happy day
with your new friend Jesus...

... and with all his other friends.

Now that you have asked Jesus
to be your friend,
there's lots to learn about him.

You can start by learning
a Bible verse about him:

"God loved the people of this world so much that he gave his only Son, so that everyone who has faith in him will have eternal life and never really die."

John 3:16